MW01037419

IF ONLY WE HAD LISTENED:

*Heaven warned Rwanda long
before the genocide*

"If I am now turning to the parish at Kibeho,
it does not mean that I am concerned only for
Kibeho or for the diocese of Butare, or for Rwanda,
or for the whole of Africa. I am concerned with
and turning to the entire world."

–Our Lady of Kibeho

IMMACULÉE ILIBAGIZA

To Mary, my Mother and the Mother of all mankind: This is for You–Happy Feast of Our Lady of Kibeho, November 28.

Praise for <u>*If Only We Had Listened*</u>

"A fascinating account of the most recent apparition of Our Lady to receive Vatican recognition. The story of Kibeho is filled with the mystery of the conflict of good and evil, of the justice and mercy of God of unanswerable questions of life leading us to take our refuge in the heart of the Holy Mother and in the hands of Divine Mercy. Like the author's other book, Left to Tell, you will never forget this book."

–**Fr. Benedict J. Groeschel, CFR**, is the founder of the community of the Franciscan Friars of the Renewal. He is the author of many books, including *Small Still Voice* and his weekly TV program airs every Sunday evening on the Eternal Word Television Network (EWTN).

Table of Contents

Foreword

What is the power of the *Word?* When we open the Bible, the living Word of God, we read that God created the world through the power of one Word. We later read in the scriptures that Christ came to this world through the same power of the created Word. His life was written on the pages of the Gospel, the Word of Life.

In Kibeho, a small village in southern Rwanda, Mary, the Mother of Jesus Christ, appeared as the Mother of the Word. This was certified by the Catholic Church in 2001. She gave us commentary on the Gospel of the Cross, which should be explored and read today as a special sign of the times. The Mother of the Word is calling us to receive this word, to come to know Jesus the Living Word, and to implement Him into our daily lives.

Some may say that there is nothing new in this message, and that Christ has already called us to conversion, to sincere prayer, to unite our sufferings with the mystery of His Cross, and to respect God's commandments. However, in today's world we often forget about these teachings, so it's important to be reminded of them. Our Mother's revelations can help bring about great transformations—starting with each of our own lives, and then by building up in the world a kingdom of peace and justice.

Just as God sent his Son on a mission of salvation, He chose Mary to be His mother. Just as Jesus chose and sent the apostles, today God is choosing and sending new apostles. Immaculée Ilibagiza and many other people are special apostles sent to work for the message of Kibeho. Immaculée is finding the time in her daily life to explore the message of Kibeho and she is trying to communicate it to the entire world. Since the apparitions were very rich and extensive, we need the patience and the perseverance to explore them to the end. The most essential messages are those of the three seers recognized by the Church. Yet in this book, we can also find some other revelations from that are recorded in various documents.

Immaculée wants to assist us on the path of the Lord and of His Mother, so that we can open our hearts and fill them up with the richness of their message. She also wants us to be accompanied on this path by the Rosary of the Seven Sorrows, which was taught by the Mother of the Word during the apparitions. Mary desires that this rosary be prayed by the faithful. It will give us greater hope on our path of taking up the cross daily, and it will transform this path into the praiseworthy road of the Risen Lord.

In a special way, my desire is that this message will bring an end to the still-swimming rivers of blood about which the message of Kibeho speaks. The tragic experience of the genocide in Rwanda should be a special warning for the world today, which is still marked by dangerous ethnic conflict, and by religious and international crises. Violence and exploitation are often the daily bread that underdeveloped nations and peoples must face. The word of the Sorrowful Mother from Kibeho is calling us to convert and to open ourselves to the gift of love, to forgive and to offer a helping hand, rather than to close our hands into destroying fists. The Beautiful Queen of Love is expressing her wish with words: "My children, please pray to Jesus and worship Him, and remember the things you have heard. Our Savior's message will lead you to Him. Live your life by His Word."

Finally, it's important to emphasize that already in 1982, the Mother of the Word told one of the visionaries, Alphonsine, that these revelations would be recognized by the Pope and would be meant for Kibeho, for Rwanda, for Africa, and for the entire world—radiating their universal message to people and doing a lot of good, not only now but also in the future. So let us find the time to hold this literary work from Immaculée in our hands, which builds on her previous work, *Our Lady of Kibeho*. I believe it will contribute to our spiritual growth and strengthen us in the battle to make the choice of good over evil.

–Father Leszek Czelusniak, MIC
Director of the Marian Formation Center "CANA" in Kibeho, Rwanda

Introduction

Only a few years ago the tiny, impoverished African village of Kibeho in my homeland of Rwanda was unknown to the world; however, it was not unknown to God. Today, like Lourdes and Fátima, Kibeho is one of the holiest pilgrimage sites and centers of sacred healing in all Christendom.

It began in 1981 when the Blessed Virgin Mary appeared to a teenaged student named Alphonsine Mumureke as she served lunch to her classmates at Kibeho's all-girl Catholic high school. Alphonsine fell into a trance as the Blessed Mother appeared in a golden ball of light and began to speak in a soft, musical voice to the dumbstruck girl. Mary told Alphonsine that she wanted to be known as the "Mother of the Word," that she loved the simple purity of Alphonsine's faith and prayers, and that she desperately wanted all of her "earthly children" to pray to her with the same amount of love and devotion.

When the brief encounter ended and Mary had ascended back to heaven, Alphonsine collapsed onto the ground in a state of semiconsciousness as her schoolmates and teachers gathered around her and demanded to know what had happened. Alphonsine confided that she had seen and spoken with the Virgin, that the Lady's beauty was so great it could not be described in words, and that the golden light radiating from the Blessed Mother was filled with the immeasurable love Mary felt for all the people in the world, whom she called her "earthly children."

As it had happened many years before and thousands of miles away with Bernadette of Lourdes and the three young visionaries to whom the Virgin appeared to in Fátima, Alphonsine's apparition of the Blessed Mother was not believed. The poor girl was dismissed as a liar and was cruelly ridiculed and mocked. But the Blessed Mother continued to appear to Alphonsine with messages of love, which she instructed the young visionary to share with her classmates. Facing even greater persecution, accusations of heresy, and threats of expulsion from school, Alphonsine prayed for the Virgin to appear to other students so they might believe what she said was true. The Virgin answered Alphonsine's prayers and soon Mary appeared to two other girls at Kibeho high school: Marie-Claire Mukangango, one of Alphonsine's most outspoken tormentors, and Anathalie Mukamazimpaka, a respected and pious girl who was believed to always speak the truth.

Soon hundreds of local peasants began milling about the school each day waiting for the Virgin to appear to one of the girls with messages from heaven. Within weeks the entire country was talking about the three visionaries and the "Miracle of Kibeho." Reports of mystical visions in the sky above Kibeho were being broadcast on Rwandan radio, and a miraculous rain fell on even the sunniest days over the crowds that gathered near the school—a rain that healed the sick and cured the lame. Soon tens of thousands of Rwandans were traveling hundreds of miles on foot to make the pilgrimage to Kibeho. Other young people also began receiving visions from the Blessed Virgin and a few were even blessed by receiving apparitions of Jesus.

The Church was alarmed by the massive crowds assembling at Kibeho and worried the miracles could be the work of the devil. The local bishop quickly launched an official investigation to scrutinize the apparitions, assembling a team of scientists, doctors, psychiatrists, and theologians who subjected the visionaries to months of rigorous physical and psychological testing. The Vatican was contacted and experts were flown in from around the world to observe the states of "ecstasy" the visionaries entered during the apparitions. Needles were stuck into the visionaries during their apparitions, burning candles were held against their skin, and bright lights were shone directly into their eyes, but none of the visionaries showed any reaction to physical pain while conversing with the Blessed Mother. In fact, each visionary reported that when the Virgin appeared before them, the crowds vanished from their view and the only thing they could see was Mary hovering about in an endless field of beautiful flowers.

The scientists and an army of journalists began recording the messages the visionaries delivered from heaven. Many more medical tests and intense interrogations of the young seers were conducted in an effort to disprove the possibility that true miracles were actually taking place in Kibeho. However, despite their combined investigations, the scientists and theologians found it impossible to deny that supernatural events were taking place in Kibeho, or to ignore the messages that were given.

The Blessed Mother entrusted each visionary with a particular message to spread to others, although they shared the common scriptural themes of prayer, fasting, penance, conversion of the heart, acceptance of our daily crosses, and preparation for Christ's return. The children shared these messages with the people who came from all parts of Rwanda and the surrounding countries. A podium was built within the schoolyard for the visionaries to stand on to help accommodate the crowds that swelled to up to twenty thousand at a time to see them.

The visions were often joyous occasions during which the Blessed Mother would encourage the visionaries to lead the multitude of pilgrims in prayer, song, and dances that celebrated the love of God. But on one ominous in day in 1982, all of the visionaries reported horrid visions of unspeakable violence, bloodshed, torture, destruction, and thousands of dismembered corpses littering the landscape—it was a prophetic warning from the Virgin Mary that if Rwandans did not cleanse their hearts of hatred and fill their souls with God's love, evil would win out and a genocide would sweep across the land. Sadly, the Virgin's warning went unheeded and in 1994, Our Lady's prediction became reality: The terrible Rwandan genocide unfolded exactly as she prophesized.

During that dark time the miracles of Kibeho were lost to the world and Rwanda suffered horribly in the aftermath of a holocaust. But slowly, as the years passed and the country began to heal, pilgrims began to return to Kibeho. At first it was only a trickle of the faithful seeking solace from their Heavenly Mother after losing their homes, their hope, and so many of their loved ones during the war. But soon hundreds, and then thousands of Rwandans began journeying to Kibeho. Rwandans from each tribe and every walk of life found that Kibeho was a place they could find forgiveness and pray together for reconciliation. Before long they were joined by pilgrims from every country in Africa and many who traveled from as far away as Europe and America. The voice of Mary was not silenced by the deeds of evil men and her love rose above Kibeho like as a beacon to the world, a signal from heaven that even in a place where darkness once held sway, God's light can always break through and touch even the most hardened or brokenhearted.

Today Kibeho is being reborn and rebuilt as a holy site and millions of pilgrims are flocking to pray at the newly constructed church and shrine honoring our Lady of Kibeho. New guest houses are being built every day to accommodate the ever-growing number of pilgrims, many of whom regularly report seeing visions of Mary and Jesus in the sky above the village. Dozens of pilgrims say they have been miraculously cured of serious diseases while praying at the blessed site.

Kibeho, a once unknown village in one of the remotest parts of the world, is now the most visited location in Rwanda. The world's largest bronze statue of Jesus' Divine Mercy towers high on a hill above Kibeho, beckoning the faithful to remember and remain true to the words and messages delivered by the Blessed Mother in this sacred place.

In 2001, after a twenty-year investigation into the events of Kibeho, the Vatican formally recognized the authenticity of the Virgin Mary's appearance to the original three visionaries: Alphonsine, Marie-Claire, and Anathalie. Kibeho has now become the only Vatican-approved Marian site on the African continent, placing the humble village on the same spiritual level with the very few officially recognized apparition sites in the world, such as Lourdes and Fátima. Although the Church has yet to authenticate any messages received by five other visionaries, none of these revelations has been contrary to the teachings of the Catholic Church, and Vatican authorities concluded that the case can be reopened at a future date. The international Christian community has experienced countless conversions and documented physical healings through the intercession of Our Lady of Kibeho, "Mother of the World." These divine graces, conversions, and miracles are a sign and reminder of the immense love that our Father in heaven has for each of us.

In a pastoral letter, Monsignor Jean-Baptiste Gahamanyi, the former Bishop of Butare, Rwanda, stated: "In the history of the Church, approved apparitions have often been a signal of alarm to invite the world to become converted. Their role has been to arouse dormant consciences to be vigilant while awaiting the coming of Christ. They have been pressing calls adapted to the spiritual climate of an era." So it is with heartfelt gratitude that we should receive and accept the messages God has sent through His Mother, during these turbulent times. They are a sign of God's mercy and grace; therefore, we must heed the warnings while there is still time for our conversion. Living Our Lord and Our Lady's messages gives us hope and makes us a light in a world submerged in darkness. We must choose God and use His gift of free will by imitating Our Lady with ceaseless prayer, penance, and fasting.

The time to repent is now! Our Lady stated, "If I am now turning to the parish at Kibeho, it does not mean that I am concerned only for Kibeho or for the diocese of Butare, or for Rwanda, or for the whole of Africa. I am concerned with and turning to the entire world." Our Lady's call continues to echo the words of her Son, "Be converted and believe in the Gospel while there is still time."

Many people have asked me "What did Our Lady say? What did Our Lord say exactly?" It is because of these requests that I wrote this book. You see, the nature of the apparition in Kibeho was a conversation between a mother and a child, between a father and a child, so in many cases the apparitions are an expression of love between a heavenly parent and an earthly child. However here and there you would hear the visionary repeating a message addressed to the population at large, word for word from Our Lady or from Our Lord. The messages contained in this book were collected over the years from conversations with the seers, from audio recordings of their admonitions from Our Lady, and from the recollections of those present during the apparitions. They have been translated from Kinyarwanda to English. As you read, pray for the descent of the Holy Spirit, that you may accept them with an open heart.

—*Immaculée*

Messages from Heaven

***Our Lady of Kibeho invites you to
strengthen and deepen your
prayer life.***

"My children, there are many who
want to pray, who try to pray, but do not
know how to pray. You must ask for the
strength and knowledge to understand
what is expected of you. My love goes out
to all of you, for there are many here who
want to reach the road to heaven, but do
not have the strength or knowledge to ask
for God's help. My children, listen to my
words, for I will teach you how to pray
from the bottom of your hearts."

"You must begin your prayers by offering God all you conceal in your soul. God sees your every action and knows your every thought, you can hide nothing from Him. But you must tell Him yourself, you must be willing and strong enough to confess all your transgressions of body, mind, and spirit to Him. Hold back nothing, admit all your bad deeds and thoughts. Then you must ask for God's forgiveness from the bottom of your heart."

"Rest assured that if you confess and seek forgiveness sincerely, He will forgive you. By beginning this way, the sins you carried will not distract you from praying sincerely. You can then speak to Him knowing that your heart is clean and your conscience clear. Pray to Him fervently, make a petition, beg His favor, ask for His blessing: God sees your heart and knows you seek His help with a repentant heart."

"Then, my children, you too must offer forgiveness by asking God to forgive all those who have trespassed against you, all who have given you suffering, insult, or injury. Forgive them in prayer and ask God to bless them and help them."

"Then pray for the spiritual and physical welfare of your relatives, for all your brothers and sisters, that God may bless them. Then give thanks to Him for having received and answered your prayers. Most important, you must ask God for the strength you need to do His will, ask for the strength not stray from His light. Pray for the courage and wisdom to walk only the road leading to heaven."

"And never forget my children, to pray for the strength to be humble. Your prayers have no meaning if they don't come from the depths of your heart, and you cannot open your heart to the Lord without humility. I love you my children. When you lack the strength to pray, ask for my help. Pray for my intercession, and I will strengthen you and bring you to my Son and to the Father through your prayer."

"Do not worry about anything, even though the one who follows Jesus may well receive poverty and unhappiness, while the one who has no time for God may receive material abundance. Know that the former will be rewarded in heaven at the end of his life, whereas the latter will be rewarded only on this earth, and will one day lose everything."

"Why are you so prematurely curious? Know and accept, rather, that you are all God's children, in union with Him, but your destiny has not yet been determined."

"Each one of you will have to give an account of what has been entrusted to you."

"If you were forbidden to continue living on this earth, where would you go?"

"Those who go to heaven are those who have struggled to get there."

"Prayer should be accompanied by deeds."

"You should all care for each other, whether rich or poor, good or bad, because Jesus lived among you all without discriminating."

"Be patient with all people, because God is patient with you."

"Do not work for the things of this world, since they do not belong to you and you will not be here forever. You are only temporary travelers."

"You who rely on your intelligence: Stop and take time to ponder that this intelligence comes from nowhere but the kindness of God. God has proved His mercy by giving you the possibility of using His creation as you wish. If He had deprived you of your own free will, He would have created all of you equal; no one would have been able to think or understand. You would have perceived, but not been able to distinguish between good and bad. Thus God has granted you freedom so that each man may choose. God shows you what is good and He shows you the true road. Choose then, with His help, the road that you wish to follow."

"Think of all that you see and do that is beyond human understanding and know that you are doing it through the will and power of God. Everything that helps you in your spiritual faculties comes from God."

"I ask you to work in order to benefit yourselves. You also work for the men you live with and you work for God. Follow the law that God has given you and that you have received and accepted willingly. Work for God, whom you have promised to serve. If you do not honor your commitments, if they remain mere words, what will you answer to God when He asks you about them? This is what will condemn you."

"You are all undertaking the same journey, so help each other, do not leave anyone on the road, in case you are asked one day, 'What are you doing here alone? Why have you left the one you were to bring with you?'"

"Those who accept this assignment, let them continue to do good without hesitation. But do not expect rewards, for there is still some way to go and you do not know how the journey will end. Each day apply yourself to do well what God asks of you."

"There are many lights in the world to follow, but there is only one true light, that of God. Live with your faith throughout your life. Don't wear it like a coat that you put on and take off, since this won't save you when you die."

"The one who turns to God in this world, and lives according to God's will, can, through Divine Mercy, shorten and even avoid his time in purgatory."

"I have come to prepare the way for Him, for your own good, and yet you do not want to accept, you do not want to understand. There is so little time remaining, yet you still allow yourselves to be distracted by earthly goods and desires, which will soon all pass away. I see so many of my children going astray, and so I come to plead with them, and to show them the correct way."

"All of you, run to me. I am the best way to Jesus."

*On June 25, 1982 Alphonsine asked
Our Lady if she had shown her any
disrespect in calling her "darling."
Our Blessed Mother answered:*

"When a child is without reproach in front of her mother, she will tell her everything that is in her heart. Although I am the Mother of God, I know how be simple and humble, how to place myself at your level in a much better way than you yourself could! Thus, I like a child who is joyful with me, because to me, this is the most beautiful sign of trust and love. All those who feel shocked by your expression do not understand the mysteries of God. So, behave like little children toward me, because I also like to express my love for you…

"...If I were cross with you, would you dare to speak to me in such a way? Let me, as your mother, embrace all my children with my love, so that they can tell me everything, as you want to! Do not be afraid of your mother, you should always love me as I love you!"

"You will tell them that I open my arms to them; he who comes to me, I will welcome and embrace him to my heart. I lovingly welcome those who are attentive to what I am showing them, and who have recourse to me, whereas others are concerned only with what will lead them nowhere."

"Tell them that I am always with them and that I will accompany them to the end of their days. I am calling you so that you will come to me, and I will lead you to my Son. But still you stand back. What is it that drives you away from this call?"

Mary, the Mother of God and our Mother, stated to Marie-Claire on March 27, 1982:

"When I visit someone and speak to them, I am openly addressing all people. If I am now turning to the parish at Kibeho, it does not mean that I am concerned only for Kibeho or for the diocese of Butare, or for Rwanda, or for the whole of Africa. I am concerned with and turning to the entire world."

The Mother of the World gave the following message to Alphonsine on November 28, 1989:

"Dear children, who I love so much: I give you all my blessing. Not only for those who have come to Kibeho, but that it may spread throughout the world."

Regarding Anathalie's mission, Mary conveyed this message to her:

"So many souls are running to ruin that I need your help to turn them back to my Son. As long as you are on earth, you have to contribute to the salvation of souls. If you will work with me, I will give you a mission to lead those lost back from the darkness. Because the world is bad, my child, you will suffer. So, if you accept this task, you must also accept all the sufferings I send you with joy, love, and patience. No one goes to heaven without suffering, and as a child of Mary, you may never put down the cross you bear."

"My daughter, you are being sent on a mission of love. You will remind the world of my Son's great mercy and the boundless love He has for His children. Tell them that He offers their souls peace and their hearts happiness beyond imagination. Plead with them to pray to their heavenly mother, for I will give them the strength they need to open their hearts to Jesus and let His love wash away their sins and despair. Tell them to accept His love, and they will receive eternal joy. Now go, my child, and preach the loving Word of the Lord."

"My child, pray your rosary while you walk. When you meet an orphan, treat him as your own child, give comfort to the troubled, and care for the sick. Never refuse any who ask for your help. If your pockets are empty, give them hope. Your every action must be born of kindness, your every word spoken with love. Live as God would have you live, and others will be inspired to do the same. By walking the world as a shepherd, you will show my earthly children that the walk to heaven is along a narrow road that is sometimes rough to travel. But the road leading to Satan is wide and easy to follow, because the devil puts no obstacles on the road to darkness."

"One looks for that which is lost. What more are you waiting for?"

"Many profess to be my friends, but few agree to really help me in my mission."

"Listen to this: Seek to honor those commitments that you have undertaken without complaining. You came freely, without being forced. So choose. Announce the message as you promised you would, and accept the travail to which you have devoted yourself. Clothe yourself in tiredness and suffering, and go help my children who are getting lost in the mud."

Messages for the Youth of the World:
In speaking to the young people, the
Virgin Mary conveyed this message:

"I wish to say to the young people that you become like beautiful flowers for me on this earth."

"A tree is straightened when still young. Children have tender hearts, while so many adults have hardened theirs until they have become surrounded by thorns."

*In this message, Jesus spoke
to young people:*

"Young people must stop treating their bodies as playthings and instruments of pleasure. So many of the youth are using any means they can to find love and to be loved by others! They have forgotten that true love comes from God and God alone. Instead of serving Him, they live at the service of money. Young women must make their bodies instruments that will glorify God, not serve as objects of pleasure for the lust of men. Young men must seek to satisfy the hunger of their spirit, not feed the desires of their flesh. Tell them all to pray to my mother to intercede on their behalf. Tell the youth not to ruin their lives; the wrong way of living can weigh heavily on their future."

The Mother of the Word gave this message to Alphonsine on November 28, 1989:

"And you young people, your youth leads you to an optimism which borders on naïveté. Everything appears effortless and attainable to you. Be watchful, be careful not to fall, since the smallest stumble could prove fatal for you."

Defeat Satan, Your Enemy: In these messages Our Blessed Mother encourages you to resist Satan:

"God loves you all, and only God's love is true and everlasting. Satan wants to destroy your souls. You must do everything in your power to resist the temptations he places in front of you, for they will only bring you to darkness."

"The one who implores the Lord will conquer, but the one who does not believe in Him will be defeated."

"The good go to heaven to live with God, and the bad go to hell with Satan. Know that it is the struggle you are daily engaged in, within the freedom you have received from God, that determines your fate."

*In praying to fight evil, Mary
gave this message:*

"The rosary is the most powerful tool of prayer and conversion to fight evil and receive God's love."

With regards to praying the rosary as a non-Catholic, Our Lady stated:

"I do not look at religion. All people are my children regardless of their beliefs. Pray the rosary, not as Catholics, but as my children."

Mary gave these messages when speaking of carrying your crosses:

"The crosses that God sends you give you more happiness than those you choose for yourselves."

"Why do you gladly accept the worldly, material privileges that God grants you, and yet you will not accept the trials that lead you to Him? Which of these ways do you reckon will lead you to God?"

"You who carry the cross without even knowing that you are doing so, accept your burden and the One for whom you are carrying it."

Our Lady of Kibeho also spoke about suffering on this earth:

"When you look at the earth, you should know that when you die you will leave everything there. Look around you. Each one has his suffering. Let this lesson inspire you to live in union with God and at peace with all men."

"What are you waiting for? You spend your time indulging yourselves in worldly pleasure, whereas eternal happiness belongs to the one who has known suffering, accepted it, and offered it up to the Lord."

"You are weeping, you are suffering, but you have a Comforter. Think about this."

"Stop clinging to all that is bothering you, to all that is depriving you of peace, and instead aim with all your strength toward the Tree of Life."

"Where there is suffering, let there be joy."

"Blessed is the one who accepts being an instrument for me, for I will reward him in heaven. All the trials he has to endure will end one day, and I will save him from many obstacles that come from men."

*On September 16, 1982, Jesus
gave this message:*

"These forthcoming times, these times that are leading up to God will be times of trials, times when each person will have to bear his own cross. The one who would follow Me will have to suffer. Any person who would take the road to heaven will walk in suffering, until the day he finds eternal rest. From that day on, he will suffer no more. However, the one who takes the road to hell will walk with no difficulty, yet he will suffer for eternity."

Here, the Queen of Peace speaks about a soul at peace:

"For all of you who have been declared incurable, nothing is healthier than a soul at peace. There is no greater wealth than that of a pure heart."

"You are burdened in life with cares of every sort. Understand that difficulties are the daily bread of all who live on this earth. When they become too hard to cope with, know how to offer them to God. He really likes and expects from every Christian at least one sacrifice."

"As for you whose homes do not guarantee the happiness that you rightly expect from them, just think of the Holy Family who lived in dire poverty and suffered the misunderstanding of the neighborhood. In all your trials entrust yourselves to the Holy Family. They will support you and protect you."

*Mary Our Mother gave this
message for priests and religious:*

"Priests, religious men and women, the sort of life you have been called to is especially demanding and comprises many difficulties. The important thing is to remain faithful to your commitment."

Regarding signs and miracles,
Our Lady of Kibeho gave these
two messages:

"Why do you insist on miracles? There are miracles every day, but you do not believe in them. Rather, ask for the light because you are blind. Learn to interpret the signs, wherever they are written, because signs are given to you every day. Happy is he who believes without waiting for miracles, since those who wait for miracles will have difficulty believing. When the miracles no longer take place, their faith will disappear."

On August 15, 1982, Our Lady shared a vision with the children, which they described as, "a river of blood, people who were killing each other, abandoned corpses with no one to bury them, a tree all in flames, bodies without heads." There was agony, torment, and inconsolable sorrow throughout the land. Although Our Lady's prophesies and warnings of the consequences of sin were shared throughout the country, the callous refused to convert and amend their lives.

Our Lady further warned that her messages were not just for Africa, but were a wake-up call for the entire world population. She reiterated that the world is trying to live without God, and that this revolt has led us to the very edge of catastrophic events. Time and again the Bible also warned of chastisements if the children of God rebelled against His laws. Just as in the Gospel of Luke, where Jesus wept over Jerusalem as they did not heed His words and recognize the time of His visitation, He now weeps for us.

As in the Gospels, the recent apparitions offer a forewarning, but how are we opening our hearts and listening to the pleas of Our Lady?

"Repent! Repent! Repent! Pray! Pray! Pray!"

Our Lady calls us unceasingly from every corner of the world. Are we listening? Will we listen? Will enough of God's children return to Him before it is too late?

***In this message to Anathalie,
Our Blessed Mother asks you to
answer her appeals:***

"I speak to you, but you do not hear. I want to lift you up, but you remain lying down. I am calling you, but your ears are closed. When are you going to do what I am asking of you? You remain indifferent to all my appeals. When are you going to understand? When are you going to show any interest in what I have been telling you? I gave you many signs, but you will not believe. How long will you remain deaf to my appeals?"

On April 2, 1982, Our Lady of Sorrows called you to repent:

"Repent! Repent! Repent! When I tell you this, I am not addressing only you, child, but I am making this appeal to all the world. Today man empties all things of their true value. Those who are continually committing sins are doing so without ever accepting that what they are doing is wrong."

She gave the following message
to Marie-Claire:

"Why do some people not believe that I have come to convert the world? I ask them to covert themselves, to abandon impurity and open their hearts to the way of Christ, but they refuse to listen and to act."

Mary, Our Mother gave this message calling you to love:

"You must love each other and not hold on to anger. Many in this country have hatred in their hearts, you must cleanse your own heart with my Son's love. Pray children, pray to me and I will help you. A small seed of anger can grow into a great tree of hatred that can block God's light and cast you into darkness. My children, please listen. You must grant forgiveness for the sins of others, and pardon those who have hurt you. Remember how much I love you, and love others the same way."

"Why are you so reluctant to serve God, and yet so willing to serve Satan with all your might, even to the extent of using trickery and deviousness to succeed?"

"Why are you turning away from God and rushing toward the fire?"

"I see that your hearts are far from God."

"I am enlightening you so that you may progress, yet you are not progressing, for when darkness surrounds you, you run toward it."

"Why do you split men into good and bad, rich and poor?"

"Why do you seek recognition from your fellow men?"

"You must fear the eyes that you cannot see."

"Each man carries his last day with him wherever he may be."

"Convert your hearts and follow my Son, Jesus."

The Virgin Mary spoke about the sin of pride in this message:

"Those who, out of pride, believe only in themselves, despite my repeated warnings, are showing their contemptuous attitude. Those who argue that such an attitude is not sinful are making God out to be a liar. I earnestly ask these people to pray for the grace to acknowledge their sin."

In these two messages, Our Blessed Mother spoke of fashion, pleasing God, and physical beauty:

"You who love to show off in flashy clothes, know that you must not try to please men, but rather to please only God. Wherever you may go, whatever you may do, in spite of your beautiful clothes, you will always be naked in front of God."

"Shame comes when everything appears in the light. Those who pride themselves on their beauty should humble themselves. Beauty comes only from God. Change your hearts and search for what can save your souls."

On December 24, 1983,
Our Lady stated:

"A stranger is someone who comes from afar and whom we do not often see. You also are a stranger in front of God, if you are far from Him, if you do not do His will, although He is calling you every day to start on your journey."

Mary gave this message on being
faithful to your vocation:

"Whether you wish to forget your vocation, or whether you are unfaithful to it, God will continue to beckon until the day when He asks you why you have not been faithful to His call."

"Love and do all you want, but do the will of God, because God has placed us on this earth to do His will."

"Those who think they are good, remember that only God is good, but the good man is the one who does God's will."

Jesus gave this message on worldly riches:

"Man is chasing the wind. Some people do not believe in the existence of heaven, they say that the only heaven is on this earth. Yet on this earth, all are poor, and all need the gifts of God. Poverty is not a lack of money, nor is it a lack of food to eat. The only real poverty is the lack of grace that leads to the Lord. The possessions of this world are only ashes. The only real riches are the riches of the heart."

Our Lady of Kibeho spoke of the necessity of prayer and conversion:

"Men do not pray enough, and among those who pray, many do not pray as they should. It is necessary to pray that they may be converted, that they change their life and return to the sacraments and in particular the Sacrament of Reconciliation; that they detach themselves from the goods of the world and look for the goods of heaven; that they humble themselves before God so that peace, mercy, and fraternal charity may reign among them."

"Dear children, pray, pray! Follow the Gospel of my Divine Son, take it for your guide, and nothing will rob you of the happiness that is in your hearts. My Son suffered terribly, was persecuted, shamefully buffeted, but in all this He did not lose His dignity as King of Heaven and Earth...

"All of you have become the butt of everyone because you like prayer. You who have been accused of self-centeredness and idleness because you follow the way of Consecration to God, I tell you, the moment will come when you will know joy."

"I speak also to those in power who have responsibilities to fulfill for others, as their representatives: Be servants of your people, not their executioners. Give a fair share to your fellow citizen of the goods that are available instead of monopolizing them for yourselves. Do not be evil, do not attempt to muzzle those who have the courage to denounce your mistakes publicly. I am telling you and I repeat it: Whatever you do in this way will be wasted work, injuring people who oppose you simply because they are set on having the rights of man respected or seeking the triumph of good or witnessing to their love of God. Everything you do will amount to nothing."

The original three visionaries at Kibeho High School in 1982.
From the left, Anathalie, Marie-Claire, and Alphonsine.

Pilgrims flock to Kibeho in the early 1980s.

Anathalie holding rosaries for the
Holy Mother to bless during an apparition.

Visionary Alphonsine is recorded during an apparition in 1982.

Visionary Stephanie during an apparition.

Visionary Segatashya during an apparition. Jesus had just told him to drink holy water on the podium to quench his spiritual thirst.

Visionary Marie-Claire during an apparition,
receiving her mission from the Blessed Mother to teach
the Rosary of the Seven Sorrows to the world.

Visionary Agnes during an apparition on the podium.

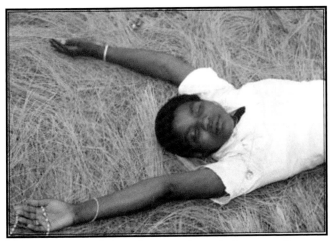

Visionary Anathalie collapses at the end of an apparition.

The first visionary, Alphonsine,
in communication with the Virgin Mary.

Alphonsine being recorded and tested by
doctors during an apparition.

Visionary Valentine during a 1992 apparition.

Pilgrims celebrating the Feast of Our Lady of Kibeho on
November 28, 2006, the 25th anniversary of the first apparition.
The yellow containers they hold are filled with
water for the Virgin Mary to bless.

Our Lady of Kibeho looks out from the shadows toward
the pilgrims gathered at her shrine in 2007.

Our Lady of Kibeho.

Pilgrims watching in wonder as the sun spins and miraculous images of the Virgin Mary and the holy cross appear in the sky above Kibeho in 2007. Miraculous visions and cures continually occur there to this day.

Here I am with Bishop Augustin Misago, who, after 20 years of investigation, approved Kibeho as a Marian apparition site in 2001. To date he has acknowledged the authenticity of the messages received by visionaries Alphonsine, Anathalie, and Marie-Claire.

The doctor who was commissioned by the Church
to test the visionaries welcomed our group and was so
grateful for all the pilgrims who had come to Kibeho.

It is so beautiful to see the Rwandan culture.

The landscape of Rwanda is breathtaking!

I can't help feeling the peace and joy of Kibeho.

Playing with the local children in Kibeho.

We took time to visit the silverback gorillas. Here I am posing with Kathy, Angelle, and our new friend!

Time spent with visionary Anathalie was
life-changing for the pilgrims.

The Chapel of the Seven Sorrows of Kibeho that was built
at the request of Our Lady of Kibeho.

One of the most amazing experiences in Rwanda
is seeing the traditional Rwandan dancers.

We visited the orphans of Rwanda, who are
being helped by Left to Tell Foundation.

After a long flight, it was a thrill to welcome the first
International Pilgrims to my homeland with open arms.

Ann and Charlotte holding the orphans
we visited on our journey.

Despite the memories of the genocide, there is much joy and a lot of dancing in Rwanda!

We spend so much time in beautiful prayer.

Our last day in Kibeho . . . our hearts were forever changed.

***In Our Lord's appearances to
Agnes, on November 6, 1982, Jesus
gave these messages:***

"Are you not happy that My Mother
and I have come to visit you?"

"Yet there are those who continue to
stray."

"There are those who are still asleep."

"There are those who remain deaf."

"There are those who have a heart of stone."

"There are those who are filled with hatred, those who are set on destroying all peace on earth."

"My Mother and I want peace."

"Tell men that I ask them to repent and convert."

"Love one another."

"Why are you so often unfaithful to My Mother and Me?"

"There are those who continually commit sins of impurity and fornication."

"Those who continually sin ignore the fact that they depend on God."

"Few people seek heavenly treasures, while those desiring the riches of this world are so many. There is but one door that opens to heaven, but the doors to the abyss are many. The roads that lead to Satan are numerous."

"So many evils are caused by money."

"Know that many things make my Mother and Me suffer. This is why we are so often sad. There are some who do know the extent of our suffering and that it is often continual these days."

"My Mother and I have loved you so immeasurably and have consoled you so many times, yet you, on the other hand, have caused us so much sorrow. We want to dry your tears, to calm your anxiety, but you yourselves only increase it."

In these messages, Jesus encourages you to choose the road that leads to God:

"My Mother and I have come to you, but you have not listened to us. Few truly listen to us."

"You are to tell mankind this: Stop taking different roads, choose only one—that of penance and detachment from worldly goods. Let the people not be tempted by what God has lent them, because one day soon God will take it all back."

"Do not covet earthly goods, and do not complain about your suffering. Do not reject the cross that I send you, but ask rather for the grace to accept it."

"The one who trusts in Me will lack nothing."

"I have loved you even to the point of surrendering My life for you on the cross."

"Follow only one road, not two. I tell you that I will welcome anyone who comes to Me. I will listen to anyone who pleads with Me. I will quench the thirst and fill the hunger of anyone who thirsts and hungers for Me."

"I will acknowledge in heaven the one who acknowledges Me on earth."

In this message, the Mother of the Word wishes to awaken you:

"I am awakening you so that you may collect what you have and purify it. Prepare yourself for the coming of the One who will come unexpectedly, and do not leave Him standing at the front door. He has a power that surpasses your intelligence and He sees even that which you want to hide from Him."

Our Lord Jesus Christ reminds you in this message to prepare yourself while there is still time:

"This world will come to an end and man must prepare himself while there is still time. When I return to the earth, the soul will find the body it had before, and then each man will present before me an account of his own life. Those who have done well will gain the reward of heaven. Those who have committed evil will automatically condemn themselves by these evil deeds, and will not even seek to appeal against this, their own judgment. Tell all men that there is not much time left. I will return soon."

To the visionary Emmanuel,
Jesus spoke on how to know the time
of His return was near:

"Today this world is full of hatred, and you will know that the time of My return is near, that I am on My way, when you hear of and see the wars of religion. Know then that I come, for nothing will be able to stop these wars. Know, too, that it will not be easy to recognize Me, but here are the signs that will help you to know that it is Me:

"I will come like a traveler, but if I walk past a deaf man, he will hear. If I walk past a blind man, he will open his eyes and see; if I walk past a mother, she will be full of joy. The one who loves me, even if he is under a bridge, I will find him. Let it not be said that one must not live on the top of a mountain, because perhaps God cannot reach this place. Even if you are under a hill, I will still find you."

"Therefore, Emmanuel, go and tell man to be ready. Let him be faithful to each word I have said. And, moreover, to those who know that I have already come once to this earth, assure them that I am on My way back … All you people who search not for heavenly treasures but who think only of your earthly goods and riches, know that you will have to account for all My words, for as I have already said once before to this world, all things will pass, but My words will never pass away. The entire project that I have planned will be realized."

"What I am asking you to do is to repent. If you say the Rosary of the Seven Sorrows and meditate on it well, you will find all the strength you need to repent of your sins and convert your heart. The world has become deaf and cannot hear the truth of the word. Today people no longer know how to apologize for the wrong they do through sin. They put the Son of God on the cross again and again...

"That is why I have come here. I have come to remind the world, and especially you here in Rwanda—where I still can find humble souls and people who are not attached to money or wealth—to hear my words with open hearts. Pray to find repentance."

"I am awakening you so that you may collect what you have and purify it. Prepare yourself for the coming of the One who will come unexpectedly, and do not leave Him standing at the front door. He has a power that surpasses your intelligence and He sees even that which you want to hide from Him."

The Rosary of the Seven Sorrows of the Virgin Mary

This rosary recalls the seven major sorrows that the Virgin Mary suffered through—albeit with love and compassion—during the life, trials, and agonizing death of her son, Jesus Christ. It's very special to the immaculate heart of the Blessed Mother, and she wants all of us to say it as often as possible.

The Rosary of the Seven Sorrows dates back to the Middle Ages, but it gained new popularity following the Marian apparitions in Kibeho, which have been approved by the Catholic Church. During Mary's apparitions to Marie-Claire Mukangango, she assigned the young visionary a mission to reintroduce this special rosary to the world. Before her untimely death, Marie-Claire did just that, traveling widely to teach it to thousands of people, who then taught it to thousands of others.

During her visitations to Kibeho, the Holy Virgin revealed that this rosary possesses immense spiritual power for those who say it sincerely. She promised that when prayed with an open and repentant heart, the rosary would win us the Lord's forgiveness for our sins and free our souls from guilt and remorse.

She also promised that over time, the rosary would develop within us a deep understanding of *why* we sin, and that knowledge would give us the wisdom and strength to change or remove any internal flaws, weaknesses of character, or personality faults causing unhappiness and keeping us from enjoying the joyous life God intended for us to live.

The Rosary of the Seven Sorrows contains all the power you need to change your life for the better, obtain peace and happiness, realize your true potential, fulfill all your dreams, and grow closer to God's light. During one of her many apparitions to Marie-Claire, the Holy Virgin suggested that it be prayed as often as possible, but especially on Tuesdays and Fridays: Tuesday being the day Mary first appeared to Marie-Claire, and Friday being the day Christ was crucified. The Blessed Mother also stressed that the Rosary of the Seven Sorrows is intended to complement—*and in no way replace*—the traditional rosary. Pray both rosaries regularly and you'll be doubly blessed!

How to Pray The Rosary of the Seven Sorrows of the Virgin Mary

The following is a description of this amazing rosary as the Virgin Mother herself taught it to Marie-Claire in Kibeho. It may be prayed aloud or contemplated silently, alone or with others; the key is for the prayers, reflections, and meditations to always come from the depths of your heart.

I speak from experience when I promise that you'll never regret learning this wonderful rosary and that you'll soon lose track of the countless blessings that praying it will bring into your life. It's my hope that more people than ever before will learn just how amazing this rosary is.

Please note that you don't necessarily need any special beads to say these prayers; just follow the diagram and instructions on the following page. (It is, however, important that when you reach each sorrowful mystery, you take a moment to meditate on the magnitude of Mary's suffering . . . and the strength of her love.)

1. On the large medal at the bottom of the rosary:
   a. Make the sign of the cross.
   b. Say the Introductory Prayer.
   c. Say the Act of Contrition.

2. For each of the next three beads, say a Hail Mary.

3. On the first small medal:
   a. Say the prayer, "Most merciful mother, remind us always about the sorrows of your son, Jesus."
   b. Meditate upon the First Sorrowful Mystery.
   c. Say the Lord's Prayer.

4. For each of the next seven beads, say a Hail Mary.

5. On the second small medal:
   a. Say the prayer, "Most merciful mother . . . "
   b. Meditate upon the Second Sorrowful Mystery.
   c. Say the Lord's Prayer.

6. For each of the next seven beads, say a Hail Mary.

7. On the third small medal:
   a. Say the prayer, "Most merciful mother . . . "
   b. Meditate upon the Third Sorrowful Mystery.
   c. Say the Lord's Prayer.

8. For each of the next seven beads, say a Hail Mary

9. On the fourth small medal:
   a. Say the prayer, "Most merciful mother . . . "
   b. Meditate upon the Fourth Sorrowful Mystery.
   c. Say the Lord's Prayer.

10. For each of the next seven beads, say a Hail Mary.

11. On the fifth small medal:
    a. Say the prayer, "Most merciful mother . . . "
    b. Meditate upon the Fifth Sorrowful Mystery.
    c. Say the Lord's Prayer.

12. For each of the next seven beads, say a Hail Mary.

13. On the sixth small medal:
    a. Say the prayer, "Most merciful mother . . . "
    b. Meditate upon the Sixth Sorrowful Mystery.
    c. Say the Lord's Prayer.

14. For each of the next seven beads, say a Hail Mary.

15. On the seventh small medal:
    a. Say the prayer, "Most merciful mother . . . "
    b. Meditate upon the Seventh Sorrowful Mystery.
    c. Say the Lord's Prayer.

16. For each of the next seven beads, say a Hail Mary.

17. Upon reaching the large medal at the bottom of the rosary:
    a. Say the prayer, "Most merciful mother . . . "
    b. Say the Concluding Prayer.
    c. Say three times: "Mary, who was conceived without sin and who suffered for us, pray for us

Make a sign of the cross; your prayers will be answered

— **Introductory Prayer:** *My God, I offer You this rosary for Your glory, so I may honor Your Holy Mother, the Blessed Virgin, so I can share and meditate upon her suffering. I humbly beg You to give me true repentance for all my sins. Give me wisdom and humility so that I may receive all the indulgences contained in this prayer.*

— **Act of Contrition:** *O my God, I am heartily sorry for having offended You, and I detest all my sins because I dread the loss of heaven and the pains of hell; but most of all because they offend You, my God, You Who are all good and deserving of all my love. I firmly resolve, with the help of Your grace, to confess my sins, to do penance, and to amend my life. Amen.*

— **Before Each Mystery, Pray:** *Most merciful mother, remind us always about the sorrows of your son, Jesus.*

1. The First Sorrowful Mystery: The Prophecy of Simeon (Luke 2:22–35)

The Blessed Virgin Mary took Jesus to the temple, as tradition demanded that all newborns be blessed in the temple before God. There, the old priest Simeon held the baby Jesus in his hands, and the Holy Spirit filled his heart. Simeon recognized Jesus as the promised Savior and held the child high toward heaven, thanking God for granting his wish that he would live long enough to behold the Messiah.

"Now Your servant may depart this life in peace, my Lord," he said. Then he looked upon Mary and proclaimed, "And you, woman, a sword of sorrow will pierce your heart because of the suffering that shall befall your child."

The Blessed Virgin knew that she had given birth to the Savior of humankind, so she immediately understood and accepted Simeon's prophecy. Although her heart was deeply touched by this favor of bearing the baby Jesus, her heart remained heavy and troubled, for she knew what had been written about the ordeals and subsequent death of the Savior. Whenever she saw her son, she was constantly reminded of the suffering he would be subjected to, and his suffering became her own.

Prayer: *Beloved Mother Mary, whose heart suffered beyond bearing because of us, teach us to suffer with you and with love, and to accept all the suffering God deems it necessary to send our way. Let us suffer, and may our*

suffering be known to God only, like yours and that of Jesus. Do not let us show our suffering to the world, so it will matter more and be used to atone for the sins of the world. You, Mother, who suffered with the Savior of the world, we offer you our suffering, and the suffering of the world, because we are your children. Join those sorrows to your own and to those of the Lord Jesus Christ, then offer them to God the Father so that He will know the one who created it. You are a mother greater than all.

2. The Second Sorrowful Mystery:
The Flight into Egypt (Matthew 2:13–15)

Mary's heart broke and her mind was greatly troubled when Joseph revealed to her the words of the angel: They were to wake up quickly and flee to Egypt because Herod wanted to kill Jesus. The Blessed Virgin hardly had time to decide what to take or leave behind; she took her child and left everything else, rushing outside before Joseph so that they could hurry as God wished. Then she said, "Even though God has power over everything, He wants us to flee with Jesus, His son. God will show us the way, and we shall arrive without being caught by the enemy."

Because the Blessed Virgin was the mother of Jesus, she loved him more than anyone else. Her heart was deeply troubled at the sight of her infant son's discomfort, and she suffered greatly because he was cold and shivering. While she and her husband were tired, sleepy, and hungry during this long travel, Mary's only thought was about the safety and comfort of her child. She feared coming face-to-face with the soldiers who had been ordered to kill Jesus because she was aware that the enemy was still in Bethlehem. Her heart remained constantly anguished during this flight. She also knew that where they were going, there would be no friendly faces to greet them.

Prayer: *Beloved Mother, who has suffered so much, give to us your courageous heart. Give us strength so that we can be brave like you and accept with love the suffering God sends our way. Help us to also accept all the suffering we inflict upon ourselves and the suffering inflicted upon us by others. Heavenly Mother, you alone purify our suffering so that we may give glory to God and save our souls.*

3. The Third Sorrowful Mystery:
The Loss of Jesus in the Temple (Luke 2:41–52)

Jesus was the only begotten son of God, but he was also Mary's child. The Blessed Virgin loved Jesus more than herself because he was her God. Compared to other children, he was most unique because he was already living as God. When Mary lost Jesus on their way back from Jerusalem, the world became so big and lonely that she believed she couldn't go on living without him, so great was her sorrow. (She felt the same pain her son felt when he was later abandoned by his apostles during the Passion.)

As the Holy Mother looked anxiously for her beloved boy, deep pain welled in her heart. She blamed herself, asking why she didn't take greater care of him. But it was not her fault; Jesus no longer needed her protection as before. What really hurt Mary was that her son had decided to stay behind without her consent. Jesus had pleased her in everything so far: He never annoyed her in any way, nor would he ever displease his parents. She knew that he always did what was necessary, however, so she never suspected him of being disobedient.

Prayer: *Beloved Mother, teach us to accept all our sufferings because of our sins and to atone for the sins of the whole world.*

4. The Fourth Sorrowful Mystery: Mary Meets Jesus on the Way to Calvary (Luke 23:27–31)

Mary witnessed Jesus carrying the heavy cross alone—the cross on which he was to be crucified. This didn't surprise the Blessed Virgin because she already knew about the approaching death of Our Lord. Noting how her son was already weakened by the numerous hard blows given by the soldiers' clubs, she was filled with anguish at his pain.

The soldiers kept hurrying and pushing him, though he had no strength left. He fell, exhausted, unable to raise himself. At that moment, Mary's eyes, so full of tender love and compassion, met her son's eyes, which were pained and covered in blood. Their hearts seemed to be sharing the load; every pain he felt, she felt as well. They knew that nothing could be done except to believe and trust in God and dedicate their suffering to Him. All they could do was put everything in God's hands.

Prayer: *Beloved Mother, so stricken with grief, help us to bear our own suffering with courage and love so that we may relieve your sorrowful heart and that of Jesus. In doing so, may we give glory to God Who gave you and Jesus to humanity. As you suffered, teach us to suffer silently and patiently. Grant unto us the grace of loving God in everything. O Mother of Sorrows, most afflicted of all mothers, have mercy on the sinners of the whole world.*

5. The Fifth Sorrowful Mystery: Mary Stands at the Foot of the Cross (John 19:25–27)

The Blessed Virgin Mary continued to climb the mount to Calvary, following behind Jesus painfully and sorrowfully, yet suffering silently. She could see him staggering and falling with the cross some more, and she witnessed her son being beaten by soldiers who pulled his hair to force him to stand up.

Despite his innocence, when Jesus reached the top of Calvary, he was ordered to confess in front of the crowd so they could laugh at him. Mary deeply felt her son's pain and humiliation, particularly when his tormentors forced him to strip off what was left of his clothing. The Blessed Virgin felt sick at heart seeing these tyrants crucifying her son naked, shaming him terribly merely to amuse the jeering crowd. (Jesus and Mary felt more disgrace than normal people did because they were holy and without sin.)

The Blessed Virgin Mary felt pain beyond bearing when Jesus was stretched out on the cross. His murderers sang merrily as they approached him with hammers and nails. They sat on him heavily so that he could not move when they spiked him to the wood. As they hammered the nails through his hands and feet, Mary felt the blows in her heart; the nails pierced her flesh as they tore into her son's body. She felt her life fading away.

As the soldiers lifted the cross to drop it into the hole they'd dug, they deliberately jerked it, causing the force of Jesus's bodily weight to tear through the flesh on his hands and expose his bone. The pain shot through his body like liquid fire. He endured three excruciating hours skewered on the cross, yet the physical pain was nothing compared to the agonizing heartache he was forced to bear seeing his mother suffering below him. Mercifully, he finally died.

Prayer: *Beloved Mother, Queen of the Martyrs, give us the courage you had in all your sufferings so that we may unite our sufferings with yours and give glory to God. Help us follow all His commandments and those of the Church so that Our Lord's sacrifice will not be in vain, and all sinners in the world will be saved.*

6. The Sixth Sorrowful Mystery: Mary Receives the Dead Body of Jesus in Her Arms (John 19:38–40)

The friends of Jesus, Joseph and Nicodemus, took down his body from the cross and placed it in the outstretched arms of the Blessed Virgin. Then Mary washed it with deep respect and love because she was his mother. She knew better than anyone else that he was God incarnate who'd taken a human body to become the Savior of all people.

Mary could see the terrifying wounds from the flogging Jesus had received while at Pilate's. His flesh had been shredded and large strips had been torn from his back. His entire body had been so lacerated that gaping wounds crisscrossed him from head to toe. Mary found that the wounds from the nails were less severe than those caused by the flogging and by carrying the cross. She was horrified at the thought that her son had managed to carry the heavy, splintered cross all the way to Calvary. She saw the circle of blood the crown of thorns had made on his forehead and, to her horror, realized that many of the barbed thorns had dug so deeply into his skull they had penetrated his brain.

Looking at her broken boy, the Holy Mother knew that his agonizing death was far worse than the torture reserved for the wickedest of criminals. As she cleaned his damaged body, she envisioned him during each stage of his short life, remembering her first look at his beautiful newborn face as the two of them lay in the manger, and every day in between, until this heartrending moment as she gently bathed his lifeless body. Her anguish was relentless as she prepared her son and Lord for burial, but she remained brave and strong, becoming the true Queen of Martyrs. As she washed her son, she prayed that everybody would know the riches of paradise and enter the gates of heaven. She prayed for every soul in the world to embrace God's love so her son's torturous death would benefit all humankind and would not have been in vain. Mary prayed for the world; she prayed for all of us.

Prayer: *We thank you, Beloved Mother, for your courage as you stood beneath your dying child to comfort him on the cross. As our Savior drew his last breath, you became a wonderful mother to all of us; you became the Blessed Mother of the world. We know that you love us more than our own earthly parents do. We implore you to be our advocate before the throne of mercy and grace so that we can truly become your children. We thank you for Jesus, our Savior and Redeemer, and we thank Jesus for giving you to us. Please pray for us, Mother.*

7. The Seventh Sorrowful Mystery: Jesus Is Placed in the Tomb (John 19:41–42)

The life of the Blessed Virgin Mary was so closely linked to that of Jesus she thought there was no reason for her to go on living any longer. Her only comfort was that his death had ended his unspeakable suffering. Our sorrowful mother, with the help of John and the holy women, devoutly placed Jesus's body in the sepulchre, and she left him there as any other dead person. She went home with great pain and tremendous sorrow; for the first time she was without him, and her loneliness was a new and bitter source of pain. Her heart had been dying since her son's heart had stopped beating, but she was certain that our Savior would soon be resurrected.

Prayer: *Most Beloved Mother, whose beauty surpassed that of all mothers, mother of mercy, mother of Jesus, and mother to us all, we are your children and we place all our trust in you. Teach us to see God in all things and all situations, even in our sufferings. Help us to understand the importance of suffering, and also to know the purpose of our suffering as God had intended it.*

You yourself were conceived and born without sin, were preserved from sin, yet you suffered more than anybody else has. You accepted suffering and pain with love and with unsurpassed courage. You stood by your son from the time he was arrested until he died. You suffered along with him, felt every pain and torment he did. You accomplished the will of God the Father; and according to

His will, you have become our savior with Jesus. We beg you, dear Mother, to teach us to do as Jesus did. Teach us to accept our cross courageously. We trust you, most merciful mother, so teach us to sacrifice for all the sinners in the world. Help us to follow in your son's footsteps, and even to be willing to lay down our lives for others.

— **Concluding Prayer:** *Queen of Martyrs, your heart suffered so much. I beg you, by the merits of the tears you shed in these terrible and sorrowful times, to obtain for me and all the sinners of the world the grace of complete sincerity and repentance. Amen.*

Three times, say: *Mary, who was conceived without sin and who suffered for us, pray for us.*

Congratulations on finishing the Rosary of the Seven Sorrows of the Virgin Mary! Now make the sign of the cross to wipe away the tears Mary shed during the Passion of Jesus, and rest assured that your prayers will be answered!

Immaculée's Letter to Every Priest, A Plea to Celebrate the Feast of Our Lady of Kibeho, November 28

Dear Father,

My name is Immaculée Ilibagiza. I am a Rwandan genocide survivor, a devout Catholic, and the author of three published books illustrating how a deep faith in God and the power of His forgiveness can triumph over even the most unimaginable evil. My first book, *Left to Tell: Discovering God Amidst the Rwandan Holocaust*, was a *New York Times* Bestseller, and its sequel, *Led By Faith: Rising From the Ashes of the Rwandan Genocide*, has recently arrived in bookstores. But it is the subject of my third book, *Our Lady of Kibeho: Mary Speaks to the World from the Heart of Africa* that fills my heart with a joy that I want to share with you, your parishioners, and the entire world.

Although the Vatican has declared the apparitions in Kibeho to be authentic, it would not surprise me if you are unfamiliar with the Blessed Mother's visitations to three Catholic schoolgirls during the early 1980s in this remote African village in my homeland of Rwanda. Few Catholics outside of Africa are aware of Our Lady of Kibeho and the many powerful messages she delivered there, which she said that were meant for the entire world.

Many times in Kibeho, Our Lady pleaded with those present to help spread the messages to the world; my book is only a small contribution to Our Lady's wish. However, it is also for that reason I beg a small favor of you—I implore you to inform your parishioners that November 28th is when the faithful celebrate the Feast Day of Our Lady of Kibeho.

This feast day has been sanctioned by the Catholic Church since 2001, when the Vatican, after 20 years of investigation, concluded that the visitations and messages from the Blessed Mother in Kibeho were genuine—as genuine as those at Lourdes, Fátima, or Guadalupe. The Holy See formally acknowledged Our Lady of Kibeho and the great spiritual fruits contained in her messages. That recognition has made Kibeho the only Vatican-approved Marian apparition site in all of Africa.

You see, dear Father, I lost my earthly family during the genocide, but I was saved by the guidance of

Our Lady, by fully embracing the great power of God's love, and during the three months I hid in a bathroom with seven other women, being hunted by killers, I did as Our Lady told us in Kibeho: I prayed the rosary non-stop, and the chaplet of Divine Mercy. It is through Her intercession that I am alive and able to forgive those who murdered my family. Today I travel the globe speaking to people about discovering God in the midst of the bloody genocide.

A major factor in the Vatican's decision to officially recognize Our Lady of Kibeho was based on the frighteningly detailed and accurate prediction the Blessed Mother made in 1981 about an unspeakable holocaust that would soon sweep across the country if Rwandans did not truly accept God's love into their hearts. She urged us to pray the rosary in each village for peace, that our country might avoid what was going to happen. Tragically, too few heeded the Lady's warning. Thirteen years later, one million innocent people were slaughtered in the exact, horrifying manner prophesized by the Blessed Mother. If we had listened to her in Rwanda, the million people who died during the genocide would be alive today, so many broken hearts wouldn't have to be, and my parents and brothers would be alive.

Despite her apocalyptic warnings about the geno-cide, most of the messages Our Lady of Kibeho delivered were truly joyous and as comforting as tender words from a loving mother. Her appearances prompted thousands of conversions, and multitudes of pilgrims found salvation through God's love, which was always in great abundance during Mary's visits to Kibeho. Her messages also provided important instructions on how best to serve God and stressed the importance of preparing for Christ's imminent return by study-ing scripture and cleansing sin from our hearts. She provided inspired lyrics for many hymns and taught us the words to forgotten prayers, such as the Rosary of the Seven Sorrows. Unlike the brief apparitions at Lourdes and Fátima, the apparitions in Kibeho lasted for up to eight hours at a time. They were occasions of great celebration in which I and thousands of others sang the songs and danced to the music Our Lady of Kibeho offered through her visionaries, that we might be better able to live in God's light and glorify his His name.

As you can see, I am driven with a great passion to share these messages with the world; for me it is both a duty and a joy. Since the Vatican's recognition of Our Lady of Kibeho, hundreds of thousands of Africans have made the pilgrimage to a newly built Church of the Seven Sorrows and the beautiful new shrine that marks the exact spot where Our Lady appeared.

Years before the site received Vatican recognition, Father Gabriel Maindron wrote the first book ever published about Kibeho. In his elegant French he expressed how profoundly moved he was by Our Lady of Kibeho, writing that, "If one day the apparitions of Kibeho are approved by the Catholic Church, they will be celebrated as the warmest, most loving visitations of Our Lady in the history of the world."

Today Kibeho is becoming a true spiritual center in the heart of Africa. Thousands of faithful Catholics from across the African continent now make a yearly pilgrimage to Kibeho to worship at the new Church of Our Lady of the Seven Sorrows and pray at the beautiful shrine marking the spot where Our Lady appeared. Today an American architect has offered to draw up plans for a basilica based on the dimensions and design Our Lady of Kibeho herself gave to one of the visionaries. I am also donating a percentage of all profits from my new book, *Our Lady of Kibeho: Mary Speaks to the World from the Heart of Africa*, to assist in the construction of what will become the Basilica of the

Queen of Africa. It is my hope the basilica will become a beacon of faith in a world in desperate need of God's Love. Please help in my quest to serve Our Lady, her Son, and Our Father, and to let that light shine a little more brightly.

As you pray for all the souls entrusted to your care, know that I will praying for you. May Our Lady of Kibeho bless you, and bless all your efforts on her behalf.

Yours in Christ,
Immaculée Ilibagiza

Acknowledgments

With all my heart, my gratitude goes to God Almighty. Thank You for giving me life, that I might offer You this little gift. To you, my earthly mom and dad, for raising me up to love Our Lady—I never knew what those prayers we said (when I used to complain!) would do in my life. Thank you, thank you.

To Kathy Lesnar, Angelle, Jill Kramer, Steve Erwin, Lionceau Simeon, Christy Salinas, Reid Tracy as always, Jenny, Katie Hammerling, Lisa Reece, Greg Amaya, Fr. Leszek, Alphonsine Mukansanga, Aimable, Nikki, and BJ, you are the heros behind the making of this book! God bless you so much more, and may Our Lady shower you with her blessings.

About Immaculée

Immaculée Ilibagiza is a living example of faith put into action. Immaculée's life was transformed dramatically during the 1994 Rwandan genocide where she and seven other women spent 91 days huddled silently together in the cramped bathroom of a local pastor's house. Immaculée entered the bathroom a vibrant, 115-pound university student with a loving family—she emerged weighing just 65 pounds to find her entire family had been brutally murdered (with the exception of one brother who had been studying out of the country).

Immaculée credits her salvage mostly to prayer and to a set of rosary beads given to her by her devout Catholic father prior to going into hiding. Anger and resentment about her situation were literally eating her alive and destroying her faith, but rather than succumbing to the rage that she felt, Immaculée instead turned to prayer. She began to pray the rosary as a way of drowning out the negativity that was building up inside her. Through prayer, she eventually found it possible, and in fact imperative, to forgive her tormentors and her family's murderers.

Immaculée's strength in her faith empowered her to stare down a man armed with a machete threatening to kill her during her escape. She also later came face to face with the killer of her mother and her brother and said the unthinkable, "I forgive you." Immaculée knew, while in hiding, that she would have to overcome immeasurable odds without her family and with her country destroyed. Fortunately, Immaculée utilized her time in that tiny bathroom to teach herself English with only the Bible and a dictionary; once freed she was able to secure a job with the United Nations.

In 1998, Immaculée immigrated to the United States where she continued her work with the UN. During this time she shared her story with co-workers and friends, who were so impacted they insisted she write it down in book form. Immaculée's first book, *Left to Tell; Discovering God Amidst the Rwandan Holocaust* (Hay House) was released in March of 2006. *Left to Tell* quickly became a *New York Times* Best Seller. To date it has been translated into fifteen languages worldwide. Immaculée recently signed a contract with MPower Pictures to produce a major motion picture about her story.

Today Immaculée is regarded as one of world's leading speakers on peace, faith, and forgiveness. She has shared her universal message with world dignitaries, schoolchildren, multinational corporations, churches, and at many conferences. Immaculée works hard to raise money for her Left to Tell Charitable Fund, which directly benefits the children orphaned by the genocide. Please visit her website: **www.immaculee.com**.

To contact Immaculée:

Address:
Immaculee Ilibagiza LLC
Grand Central Station
New York, NY 100163

Phone: 1-507-360-0223

Websites:
www.immaculee.com
www.lefttotell.com

E-mail:
immaculee2kibeho@yahoo.com